the best
loved
poems *of*
john
betjeman

OTHER VERSE VOLUMES

Collected Poems
(new enlarged edition)

The Illustrated Poems of John Betjeman
With David Gentleman

Summoned by Bells
(verse autobiography)

The Illustrated Summoned by Bells
With Hugh Casson

Church Poems
Illustrated by John Piper

OTHER BOOKS BY OR ABOUT JOHN BETJEMAN

In Praise of Churches
(prose and verse)
With Paul Hogarth

Betjeman's Cornwall

Young Betjeman
Bevis Hillier's authorised biography
(from 1906 to 1933)

John Betjeman: New Fame, New Love
Bevis Hillier's authorised biography
(from 1934 to 1958)

John Betjeman: Letters 1926–1951
Edited by Candida Lycett Green
(Methuen)

John Betjeman: Letters 1952–1984
Edited by Candida Lycett Green
(Methuen)

Coming Home: Selected Prose of Sir John Betjeman
Edited by Candida Lycett Green
(Methuen)

John Betjeman
Read by John Betjeman and Nigel Hawthorne
(Hodder & Stoughton Audio Books)

the best
loved
poems *of*
john
betjeman

JOHN MURRAY

© The Estate of John Betjeman 1955, 1958, 1962, 1964, 1968, 1970, 1979,
1981, 1982, 2001

First published in 2003 by John Murray (Publishers)
A division of Hodder Headline

3   5   7   9   10   8   6   4   2

The moral right of the author has been asserted

A CIP catalogue record for this title is available from the British Library

ISBN 0-7195-6545 6

Typeset in 10/12.5 Plantin Light by
Servis Filmsetting Ltd, Manchester

Printed and bound in Great Britain by Clays Ltd, St Ives plc

John Murray (Publishers)
338 Euston Road
London
NW1 3BH

CONTENTS

PUBLISHER'S NOTE

John Betjeman was one of the most successful poets of all time, successful not only in that his verse is read by so many (altogether, about three million volumes have been bought so far) but also in that the world he created – or perhaps it would be truer to say revealed – is unique to him and instantly recognizable. The mention of his name alone is enough to bring to mind places such as Metroland or Cornwall, the city or country churches, the railway stations and Victorian buildings, or the dim and unheroic suburb-dwellers whose qualities he was the first to reveal in verse. He found, as no other poet did, the numinous in the ordinary, so that the ordinary has never seemed the same again.

Any collection of best-loved poems must to some extent be arbitrary. Not everyone loves the same ones best. This selection includes those most often quoted and anthologized, and it includes as wide as possible a range of Betjeman's styles and moods. He was not a satirist but there are some satires here; he could be supremely funny about things he took supremely seriously; he was often angry, especially about doctrinaire planning, or destruction or greed; he could be melancholy or apprehensive – especially about death, which filled him with awe as it did Dr Johnson.

This selection is intended above all to be enjoyable – enjoyable for those who need a reminder of the sheer pleasure John Betjeman could provide, and enjoyable too for those lucky enough to be reading him for the first time.

A SUBALTERN'S LOVE-SONG

Miss J. Hunter Dunn, Miss J. Hunter Dunn,
Furnish'd and burnish'd by Aldershot sun,
What strenuous singles we played after tea,
We in the tournament – you against me!

Love-thirty, love-forty, oh! weakness of joy,
The speed of a swallow, the grace of a boy,
With carefullest carelessness, gaily you won,
I am weak from your loveliness, Joan Hunter Dunn.

Miss Joan Hunter Dunn, Miss Joan Hunter Dunn,
How mad I am, sad I am, glad that you won.
The warm-handled racket is back in its press,
But my shock-headed victor, she loves me no less.

Her father's euonymus shines as we walk,
And swing past the summer-house, buried in talk,
And cool, the verandah that welcomes us in
To the six-o'clock news and a lime-juice and gin.

The scent of the conifers, sound of the bath,
The view from my bedroom of moss-dappled path,
As I struggle with double-end evening tie,
For we dance at the Golf Club, my victor and I.

On the floor of her bedroom lie blazer and shorts
And the cream-coloured walls are be-trophied with sports,
And westering, questioning settles the sun
On your low-leaded window, Miss Joan Hunter Dunn.

The Hillman is waiting, the light's in the hall,
The pictures of Egypt are bright on the wall,
My sweet, I am standing beside the oak stair
And there on the landing's the light on your hair.

By roads 'not adopted', by woodlanded ways,
She drove to the club in the late summer haze,
Into nine-o'clock Camberley, heavy with bells
And mushroomy, pine-woody, evergreen smells.

Miss Joan Hunter Dunn, Miss Joan Hunter Dunn,
I can hear from the car-park the dance has begun.
Oh! full Surrey twilight! importunate band!
Oh! strongly adorable tennis-girl's hand!

Around us are Rovers and Austins afar,
Above us, the intimate roof of the car,
And here on my right is the girl of my choice,
With the tilt of her nose and the chime of her voice,

And the scent of her wrap, and the words never said,
And the ominous, ominous dancing ahead.
We sat in the car park till twenty to one
And now I'm engaged to Miss Joan Hunter Dunn.

BRISTOL

Green upon the flooded Avon shone the after-storm-wet-sky
Quick the struggling withy branches let the leaves of autumn fly
And a star shone over Bristol, wonderfully far and high.

Ringers in an oil-lit belfry – Bitton? Kelston? who shall say? –
Smoothly practising a plain course, caverned out the dying day
As their melancholy music flooded up and ebbed away.

Then all Somerset was round me and I saw the clippers ride,
High above the moonlit houses, triple-masted on the tide,
By the tall embattled church-towers of the Bristol waterside.

And an undersong to branches dripping into pools and wells
Out of multitudes of elm trees over leagues of hills and dells
Was the mathematic pattern of a plain course on the bells.*

```
*1 2 2 4 4 5 5 3 3 1 1
 2 1 4 2 5 4 3 5 1 3 2
 3 4 1 5 2 3 4 1 5 2 3
 4 3 5 1 3 2 1 4 2 5 4
 5 5 3 3 1 1 2 2 4 4 5
```

DEATH IN LEAMINGTON

She died in the upstairs bedroom
    By the light of the ev'ning star
That shone through the plate glass window
    From over Leamington Spa.

Beside her the lonely crochet
    Lay patiently and unstirred,
But the fingers that would have work'd it
    Were dead as the spoken word.

And Nurse came in with the tea-things
    Breast high 'mid the stands and chairs –
But Nurse was alone with her own little soul,
    And the things were alone with theirs.

She bolted the big round window,
    She let the blinds unroll,
She set a match to the mantle,
    She covered the fire with coal.

And 'Tea!' she said in a tiny voice
    'Wake up! It's nearly *five*.'
Oh! Chintzy, chintzy cheeriness,
    Half dead and half alive!

Do you know that the stucco is peeling?
    Do you know that the heart will stop?
From those yellow Italianate arches
    Do you hear the plaster drop?

Nurse looked at the silent bedstead,
  At the gray, decaying face,
As the calm of a Leamington ev'ning
  Drifted into the place.

She moved the table of bottles
  Away from the bed to the wall;
And tiptoeing gently over the stairs
  Turned down the gas in the hall.

THE 'VARSITY STUDENTS' RAG

I'm afraid the fellows in Putney rather wish they had
The social ease and manners of a 'varsity undergrad,
For tho' they're awf'lly decent and up to a lark as a rule
You want to have the 'varsity touch after a public school.

CHORUS :
    We had a rag at Monico's. *We* had a rag at the Troc.,
    And the one we had at the Berkeley gave the customers
                                    quite a shock.
    Then we went to the Popular, and after that – oh my!
    I wish you'd seen the rag we had in the Grill Room at the
                                       Cri.

I started a rag in Putney at our Frothblower's Branch down
                                      there;
We got in a damn'd old lorry and drove to Trafalgar Square;
And we each had a couple of toy balloons and made the hell
                                     of a din,
And I saw a bobby at Parson's Green who looked like running
                                     us in.

CHORUS : We, etc.

But that's nothing to the rag we had at the college the other
                                     night;
We'd gallons and gallons of cider – and I got frightfully tight.
And then we smash'd up ev'rything, and what was the funniest
                                     part
We smashed some rotten old pictures which were priceless
                                    works of art.

CHORUS : We, etc.

There's something about a 'varsity man that distinguishes him
                                                      from a cad:
You can tell by his tie and blazer he's a 'varsity undergrad,
And you know that he's always ready and up to a bit of a lark,
With a toy balloon and a whistle and some cider after dark.

    CHORUS : We, etc.

THE ARREST OF OSCAR WILDE
AT THE CADOGAN HOTEL

He sipped at a weak hock and seltzer
    As he gazed at the London skies
Through the Nottingham lace of the curtains
    Or was it his bees-winged eyes?

To the right and before him Pont Street
    Did tower in her new built red,
As hard as the morning gaslight
    That shone on his unmade bed,

'I want some more hock in my seltzer,
    And Robbie, please give me your hand –
Is this the end or beginning?
    How can I understand?

'So you've brought me the latest *Yellow Book*:
    And Buchan has got in it now:
Approval of what is approved of
    Is as false as a well-kept vow.

'More hock, Robbie – where is the seltzer?
    Dear boy, pull again at the bell!
They are all little better than *cretins*,
    Though this *is* the Cadogan Hotel.

'One astrakhan coat is at Willis's –
    Another one's at the Savoy:
Do fetch my morocco portmanteau,
    And bring them on later, dear boy.'

A thump, and a murmur of voices –
    ('Oh why must they make such a din?')
As the door of the bedroom swung open
    And TWO PLAIN CLOTHES POLICEMEN came in:

'Mr. Woilde, we 'ave come for tew take yew
    Where felons and criminals dwell:
We must ask yew tew leave with us quoietly
    For this *is* the Cadogan Hotel.'

He rose, and he put down *The Yellow Book*.
    He staggered – and, terrible-eyed,
He brushed past the palms on the staircase
    And was helped to a hansom outside.

WESTGATE-ON-SEA

Hark, I hear the bells of Westgate,
  I will tell you what they sigh,
Where those minarets and steeples
  Prick the open Thanet sky.

Happy bells of eighteen-ninety,
  Bursting from your freestone tower!
Recalling laurel, shrubs and privet,
  Red geraniums in flower.

Feet that scamper on the asphalt
  Through the Borough Council grass,
Till they hide inside the shelter
  Bright with ironwork and glass,

Striving chains of ordered children
  Purple by the sea-breeze made,
Striving on to prunes and suet
  Past the shops on the Parade.

Some with wire around their glasses,
  Some with wire across their teeth,
Writhing frames for running noses
  And the drooping lip beneath.

Church of England bells of Westgate!
  On this balcony I stand,
White the woodwork wriggles round me,
  Clock towers rise on either hand.

For me in my timber arbour
  You have one more message yet,
'Plimsolls, plimsolls in the summer,
  Oh goloshes in the wet!'

HOW TO GET ON IN SOCIETY

Phone for the fish-knives, Norman
   As Cook is a little unnerved;
You kiddies have crumpled the serviettes
   And I must have things daintily served.

Are the requisites all in the toilet?
   The frills round the cutlets can wait
Till the girl has replenished the cruets
   And switched on the logs in the grate.

It's ever so close in the lounge, dear,
   But the vestibule's comfy for tea
And Howard is out riding on horseback
   So do come and take some with me.

Now here is a fork for your pastries
   And do use the couch for your feet;
I know what I wanted to ask you –
   Is trifle sufficient for sweet?

Milk and then just as it comes dear?
   I'm afraid the preserve's full of stones;
Beg pardon, I'm soiling the doileys
   With afternoon tea-cakes and scones.

OUR PADRE

Our padre is an old sky pilot
   Severely now they've clipped his wings,
But still the flagstaff in the Rect'ry garden
   Points to Higher Things.

Still he has got a hearty handshake;
   Still he wears his medals and a stole;
His voice would reach to Heaven, *and* make
   The Rock of Ages Roll.

He's too sincere to join the high church
   Worshipping idols for the Lord,
And, though the lowest church is my church,
   Our padre's Broad.

Our padre is an old sky pilot,
   He's tied a reef knot round my heart,
We'll be rocked up to Heaven on a rare old tune –
   Come on – take part!

CHORUS
(*Sung*) Pull for the shore, sailor, pull for the shore!
   Heed not the raging billow, bend to the oar!
Bend to the oar before the padre!
   Proud, with the padre rowing stroke!
Good old padre! God for the services!
   Row like smoke!

SLOUGH

Come, friendly bombs, and fall on Slough
It isn't fit for humans now,
There isn't grass to graze a cow
    Swarm over, Death!

Come, bombs, and blow to smithereens
Those air-conditioned, bright canteens,
Tinned fruit, tinned meat, tinned milk, tinned beans
    Tinned minds, tinned breath.

Mess up the mess they call a town –
A house for ninety-seven down
And once a week a half-a-crown
    For twenty years,

And get that man with double chin
Who'll always cheat and always win,
Who washes his repulsive skin
    In women's tears,

And smash his desk of polished oak
And smash his hands so used to stroke
And stop his boring dirty joke
    And make him yell.

But spare the bald young clerks who add
The profits of the stinking cad;
It's not their fault that they are mad,
    They've tasted Hell.

It's not their fault they do not know
The birdsong from the radio,
It's not their fault they often go
         To Maidenhead

And talk of sports and makes of cars
In various bogus Tudor bars
And daren't look up and see the stars
         But belch instead.

In labour-saving homes, with care
Their wives frizz out peroxide hair
And dry it in synthetic air
         And paint their nails.

Come, friendly bombs, and fall on Slough
To get it ready for the plough.
The cabbages are coming now;
         The earth exhales.

TREBETHERICK

We used to picnic where the thrift
    Grew deep and tufted to the edge;
We saw the yellow foam-flakes drift
    In trembling sponges on the ledge
Below us, till the wind would lift
    Them up the cliff and o'er the hedge.
Sand in the sandwiches, wasps in the tea,
Sun on our bathing-dresses heavy with the wet,
Squelch of the bladder-wrack waiting for the sea,
Fleas round the tamarisk, an early cigarette.

From where the coastguard houses stood
    One used to see, below the hill,
The lichened branches of a wood
    In summer silver-cool and still;
And there the Shade of Evil could
    Stretch out at us from Shilla Mill.
Thick with sloe and blackberry, uneven in the light,
Lonely ran the hedge, the heavy meadow was remote,
The oldest part of Cornwall was the wood as black as night,
And the pheasant and the rabbit lay torn open at the throat.

But when a storm was at its height,
    And feathery slate was black in rain,
And tamarisks were hung with light
    And golden sand was brown again,
Spring tide and blizzard would unite
    And sea came flooding up the lane.
Waves full of treasure then were roaring up the beach,
Ropes round our mackintoshes, waders warm and dry,
We waited for the wreckage to come swirling into reach,
Ralph, Vasey, Alastair, Biddy, John and I.

Then roller into roller curled
    And thundered down the rocky bay,
And we were in a water-world
    Of rain and blizzard, sea and spray,
And one against the other hurled
    We struggled round to Greenaway.
Blesséd be St. Enodoc, blesséd be the wave,
Blesséd be the springy turf, we pray, pray to thee,
Ask for our children all the happy days you gave
To Ralph, Vasey, Alastair, Biddy, John and me.

ARCHIBALD

The bear who sits above my bed
   A doleful bear he is to see;
From out his drooping pear-shaped head
   His woollen eyes look into me.
He has no mouth, but seems to say:
'They'll burn you on the Judgment Day.'

Those woollen eyes, the things they've seen
   Those flannel ears, the things they've heard –
Among horse-chestnut fans of green,
   The fluting of an April bird,
And quarrelling downstairs until
Doors slammed at Thirty One West Hill.

The dreaded evening keyhole scratch
   Announcing some return below,
The nursery landing's lifted latch,
   The punishment to undergo
Still I could smooth those half-moon ears
And wet that forehead with my tears.

Whatever rush to catch a train,
   Whatever joy there was to share
Of sounding sea-board, rainbowed rain,
   Or seaweed-scented Cornish air,
Sharing the laughs, you still were there,
You ugly, unrepentant bear.

When nine, I hid you in a loft
    And dared not let you share my bed;
My father would have thought me soft,
    Or so at least my mother said.
She only then our secret knew,
And thus my guilty passion grew.

The bear who sits above my bed
    More agèd now he is to see,
His woollen eyes have thinner thread,
    But still he seems to say to me,
In double-doom notes, like a knell:
'You're half a century nearer Hell.'

Self-pity shrouds me in a mist,
    And drowns me in my self-esteem.
The freckled faces I have kissed
    Float by me in a guilty dream.
The only constant, sitting there,
Patient and hairless, is a bear.

And if an analyst one day
    Of school of Adler, Jung or Freud
Should take this agèd bear away,
    Then, oh my God, the dreadful void!
Its draughty darkness could but be
Eternity, Eternity.

THE OLD LAND DOG
AFTER HENRY NEWBOLT

Old General Artichoke lay bloated on his bed,
    Just like the Fighting Téméraire.
Twelve responsive daughters were gathered round his head
    And each of them was ten foot square.

Old General Artichoke he didn't want to die:
He never understood the truth and that perhaps was why
It wouldn't be correct to say he always told a lie.
    Womenfolk of England, oh beware!

'Fetch me down my rifle – it is hanging in the hall'
    Just like the Fighting Téméraire;
'Lydia, get my cartridge cases, twenty-four in all',
    And each of them is ten foot square.

'I'll tell you all in detail, girls, my every campaign
In Tuscany, Bolivia, Baluchistan and Spain;
And when I've finished telling you, I'll tell you all again;'
    Womenfolk of England, oh beware!

Old General Artichoke he's over eighty-two,
    Just like the Fighting Téméraire.
His daughters all make rush mats when they've nothing else to do,
    And each of them is ten foot square.

Now all ye pension'd army men from Tunbridge Wells to Perth,
Here's to General Artichoke, the purplest man on earth!
Give three loud cheers for Cheltenham, the city of his birth.
    Womenfolk of England, oh beware!

OXFORD: SUDDEN ILLNESS
AT THE BUS-STOP

At the time of evening when cars run sweetly,
  Syringas blossom by Oxford gates.
In her evening velvet with a rose pinned neatly
  By the distant bus-stop a don's wife waits.

From that wide bedroom with its two branched lighting
  Over her looking-glass, up or down,
When sugar was short and the world was fighting
  She first appeared in that velvet gown.

What forks since then have been slammed in places?
  What peas turned out from how many a tin?
From plate-glass windows how many faces
  Have watched professors come hobbling in?

Too much, too many! so fetch the doctor,
  This dress has grown such a heavier load
Since Jack was only a Junior Proctor,
  And rents were lower in Rawlinson Road.

FALSE SECURITY

I remember the dread with which I at a quarter past four
Let go with a bang behind me our house front door
And, clutching a present for my dear little hostess tight,
Sailed out for the children's party into the night
Or rather the gathering night. For still some boys
In the near municipal acres were making a noise
Shuffling in fallen leaves and shouting and whistling
And running past hedges of hawthorn, spikey and
                                                    bristling.
And black in the oncoming darkness stood out the trees
And pink shone the ponds in the sunset ready to freeze
And all was still and ominous waiting for dark
And the keeper was ringing his closing bell in the park
And the arc lights started to fizzle and burst into mauve
As I climbed West Hill to the great big house in The
                                                    Grove,
Where the children's party was and the dear little hostess.
But halfway up stood the empty house where the ghost is
I crossed to the other side and under the arc
Made a rush for the next kind lamp-post out of the dark
And so to the next and the next till I reached the top
Where the Grove branched off to the left. Then ready to
                                                    drop
I ran to the ironwork gateway of number seven
Secure at last on the lamplit fringe of Heaven.
Oh who can say how subtle and safe one feels
Shod in one's children's sandals from Daniel Neal's,
Clad in one's party clothes made of stuff from Heal's?
And who can still one's thrill at the candle shine
On cakes and ices and jelly and blackcurrant wine,
And the warm little feel of my hostess's hand in mine?
Can I forget my delight at the conjuring show?
And wasn't I proud that I was the last to go?

Too overexcited and pleased with myself to know
That the words I heard my hostess's mother employ
To a guest departing, would ever diminish my joy,
I WONDER WHERE JULIA FOUND THAT STRANGE, RATHER
                                        COMMON LITTLE BOY?

MYFANWY

Kind o'er the *kinderbank* leans my Myfanwy,
    White o'er the play-pen the sheen of her dress,
Fresh from the bathroom and soft in the nursery
    Soap-scented fingers I long to caress.

Were you a prefect and head of your dormit'ry?
    Were you a hockey girl, tennis or gym?
Who was your favourite? Who had a crush on you?
    Which were the baths where they taught you to swim?

Smooth down the Avenue glitters the bicycle,
    Black-stockinged legs under navy-blue serge,
Home and Colonial, *Star,* International,
    Balancing bicycle leant on the verge.

Trace me your wheel-tracks, you fortunate bicycle,
    Out of the shopping and into the dark,
Back down the Avenue, back to the pottingshed,
    Back to the house on the fringe of the park.

Golden the light on the locks of Myfanwy,
    Golden the light on the book on her knee,
Finger-marked pages of Rackham's Hans Andersen,
    Time for the children to come down to tea.

Oh! Fuller's angel-cake, Robertson's marmalade,
    Liberty lampshade, come, shine on us all,
My! what a spread for the friends of Myfanwy
    Some in the alcove and some in the hall.

Then what sardines in the half-lighted passages!
    Locking of fingers in long hide-and-seek.
You will protect me, my silken Myfanwy,
    Ringleader, tom-boy, and chum to the weak.

MYFANWY AT OXFORD

Pink may, double may, dead laburnum
  Shedding an Anglo-Jackson shade,
Shall we ever, my staunch Myfanwy,
  Bicycle down to North Parade?
Kant on the handle-bars, Marx in the saddlebag,
  Light my touch on your shoulder-blade.

Sancta Hilda, Myfanwyatia
  Evansensis – I hold your heart,
Willowy banks of a willowy Cherwell a
  Willowy figure with lips apart,
Strong and willowy, strong to pillow me,
  Gold Myfanwy, kisses and art.

Tubular bells of tall St. Barnabas,
  Single clatter above St. Paul,
Chasuble, acolyte, incense-offering,
  Spectacled faces held in thrall.
There in the nimbus and Comper tracery
  Gold Myfanwy blesses us all.

Gleam of gas upon Oxford station,
  Gleam of gas on her straight gold hair,
Hair flung back with an ostentation,
  Waiting alone for a girl friend there.
Second in Mods and a Third in Theology
  Come to breathe again Oxford air.

Her Myfanwy as in Cadena days,
    Her Myfanwy, a schoolgirl voice,
Tentative brush of a cheek in a cocoa crush,
    Coffee and Ulysses, Tennyson, Joyce,
Alpha-minded and other dimensional,
    Freud or Calvary? Take your choice.

Her Myfanwy? *My* Myfanwy.
    Bicycle bells in a Boar's Hill Pine,
Stedman Triple from All Saints' steeple,
    Tom and his hundred and one at nine,
Bells of Butterfield, caught in Keble,
    Sally and backstroke answer '*Mine!*'

THE COCKNEY AMORIST

Oh when my love, my darling,
    You've left me here alone,
I'll walk the streets of London
    Which once seemed all our own.

The vast suburban churches
    Together we have found:
The ones which smelt of gaslight
    The ones in incense drown'd;
I'll use them now for praying in
    And not for looking round.

No more the Hackney Empire
    Shall find us in its stalls
When on the limelit crooner
    The thankful curtain falls,
And soft electric lamplight
    Reveals the gilded walls.

I will not go to Finsbury Park
    The putting course to see
Nor cross the crowded High Road
    To Williamsons' to tea,
For these and all the other things
    Were part of you and me.

I love you, oh my darling,
    And what I can't make out
Is why since you have left me
    I'm somehow still about.

IN WESTMINSTER ABBEY

Let me take this other glove off
   As the *vox humana* swells,
And the beauteous fields of Eden
   Bask beneath the Abbey bells.
Here, where England's statesmen lie,
Listen to a lady's cry.

Gracious Lord, oh bomb the Germans.
   Spare their women for Thy Sake,
And if that is not too easy
   We will pardon Thy Mistake.
But, gracious Lord, whate'er shall be,
Don't let anyone bomb me.

Keep our Empire undismembered
   Guide our Forces by Thy Hand,
Gallant blacks from far Jamaica,
   Honduras and Togoland;
Protect them Lord in all their fights,
And, even more, protect the whites.

Think of what our Nation stands for,
   Books from Boots' and country lanes,
Free speech, free passes, class distinction,
   Democracy and proper drains.
Lord, put beneath Thy special care
One-eighty-nine Cadogan Square.

Although dear Lord I am a sinner,
   I have done no major crime;
Now I'll come to Evening Service
   Whensoever I have the time.
So, Lord, reserve for me a crown,
And do not let my shares go down.

I will labour for Thy Kingdom,
   Help our lads to win the war,
Send white feathers to the cowards
   Join the Women's Army Corps,
Then wash the Steps around Thy Throne
In the Eternal Safety Zone.

Now I feel a little better,
   What a treat to hear Thy Word,
Where the bones of leading statesmen,
   Have so often been interr'd.
And now, dear Lord, I cannot wait
Because I have a luncheon date.

DEATH OF KING GEORGE V

'New King arrives in his capital by air . . .' *Daily Newspaper.*

Spirits of well-shot woodcock, partridge, snipe
    Flutter and bear him up the Norfolk sky:
In that red house in a red mahogany book-case
    The stamp collection waits with mounts long dry.

The big blue eyes are shut which saw wrong clothing
    And favourite fields and coverts from a horse;
Old men in country houses hear clocks ticking
    Over thick carpets with a deadened force;

Old men who never cheated, never doubted,
    Communicated monthly, sit and stare
At the new suburb stretched beyond the run-way
    Where a young man lands hatless from the air.

A SHROPSHIRE LAD

N.B. – This should be recited with a Midland accent.

Captain Webb, the swimmer and a relation of Mary Webb by
marriage, was born at Dawley in an industrial district in Salop.

The gas was on in the Institute,[1]
   The flare was up in the gym,
A man was running a mineral line,
   A lass was singing a hymn,
When Captain Webb the Dawley man,
   Captain Webb from Dawley,
Came swimming along the old canal
   That carried the bricks to Lawley.
      Swimming along –
      Swimming along –
      Swimming along from Severn,
And paying a call at Dawley Bank while swimming
                   along to Heaven.

The sun shone low on the railway line
   And over the bricks and stacks,
And in at the upstairs windows
   Of the Dawley houses' backs,
When we saw the ghost of Captain Webb,
   Webb in a water sheeting,
Come dripping along in a bathing dress
   To the Saturday evening meeting.
      Dripping along –
      Dripping along –
      To the Congregational Hall;
Dripping and still he rose over the sill and faded
                   away in a wall.

[1] 'The Institute was radiant with gas.' Ch. XIX, *Boyhood*.
A novel in verse by Rev. E. E. Bradford, D.D.

There wasn't a man in Oakengates
    That hadn't got hold of the tale,
And over the valley in Ironbridge,
    And round by Coalbrookdale,
How Captain Webb the Dawley man,
    Captain Webb from Dawley,
Rose rigid and dead from the old canal
    That carries the bricks to Lawley.
        Rigid and dead –
        Rigid and dead –
        To the Saturday congregation,
Paying a call at Dawley Bank on his way to his
                                    destination.

EXECUTIVE

I am a young executive. No cuffs than mine are cleaner;
I have a Slimline brief-case and I use the firm's Cortina.
In every roadside hostelry from here to Burgess Hill
The *maîtres d'hôtel* all know me well and let me sign the bill.

You ask me what it is I do. Well actually, you know,
I'm partly a liaison man and partly P. R.O.
Essentially I integrate the current export drive
And basically I'm viable from ten o'clock till five.

For vital off-the-record work – that's talking transport-wise –
I've a scarlet Aston-Martin – and does she go? She flies!
Pedestrians and dogs and cats – we mark them down for
                                                    slaughter.
I also own a speed-boat which has never touched the water.

She's built of fibre-glass, of course. I call her 'Mandy Jane'
After a bird I used to know – No soda, please, just plain –
And how did I acquire her? Well to tell you about that
And to put you in the picture I must wear my other hat.

I do some mild developing. The sort of place I need
Is a quiet country market town that's rather run to seed.
A luncheon and a drink or two, a little *savoir faire* –
I fix the Planning Officer, the Town Clerk and the Mayor.

And if some preservationist attempts to interfere
A 'dangerous structure' notice from the Borough Engineer
Will settle any buildings that are standing in our way –
The modern style, sir, with respect, has really come to stay.

BUSINESS GIRLS

From the geyser ventilators
    Autumn winds are blowing down
On a thousand business women
    Having baths in Camden Town.

Waste pipes chuckle into runnels,
    Steam's escaping here and there,
Morning trains through Camden cutting
    Shake the Crescent and the Square.

Early nip of changeful autumn,
    Dahlias glimpsed through garden doors,
At the back precarious bathrooms
    Jutting out from upper floors;

And behind their frail partitions
    Business women lie and soak,
Seeing through the draughty skylight
    Flying clouds and railway smoke.

Rest you there, poor unbelov'd ones,
    Lap your loneliness in heat.
All too soon the tiny breakfast,
    Trolley-bus and windy street!

CALVINISTIC EVENSONG

The six bells stopped, and in the dark I heard
Cold silence wait the Calvinistic word;
For Calvin now the soft oil lamps are lit
Hands on their hymnals six old women sit.
Black gowned and sinister, he now appears
Curate-in-charge of aged parish fears.
Let, unaccompanied, that psalm begin
Which deals most harshly with the fruits of sin!
Boy! pump the organ! let the anthem flow
With promise for the chosen saints below!
Pregnant with warning the globed elm trees wait
Fresh coffin-wood beside the churchyard gate.
And that mauve hat three cherries decorate
Next week shall topple from its trembling perch
While wet fields reek like some long empty church.

UPPER LAMBOURNE

Up the ash-tree climbs the ivy,
    Up the ivy climbs the sun,
With a twenty-thousand pattering
    Has a valley breeze begun,
Feathery ash, neglected elder,
    Shift the shade and make it run –

Shift the shade toward the nettles,
    And the nettles set it free
To streak the stained Carrara headstone
    Where, in nineteen-twenty-three,
He who trained a hundred winners
    Paid the Final Entrance Fee.

Leathery limbs of Upper Lambourne,
    Leathery skin from sun and wind,
Leathery breeches, spreading stables,
    Shining saddles left behind –
To the down the string of horses
    Moving out of sight and mind.

Feathery ash in leathery Lambourne
    Waves above the sarsen stone,
And Edwardian plantations
    So coniferously moan
As to make the swelling downland,
    Far-surrounding, seem their own.

POT POURRI FROM A SURREY GARDEN

Miles of pram in the wind and Pam in the gorse track,
   Coco-nut smell of the broom, and a packet of Weights
Press'd in the sand. The thud of a hoof on a horse-track –
      A horse-riding horse for a horse-track –
      Conifer county of Surrey approached
   Through remarkable wrought-iron gates.

Over your boundary now, I wash my face in a bird-bath,
   Then which path shall I take? that over there by the pram?
Down by the pond! or – yes, I will take the slippery third path,
      Trodden away with gym shoes,
      Beautiful fir-dry alley that leads
   To the bountiful body of Pam.

Pam, I adore you, Pam, you great big mountainous sports girl,
   Whizzing them over the net, full of the strength of five:
That old Malvernian brother, you zephyr and khaki shorts girl,
      Although he's playing for Woking,
      Can't stand up
   To your wonderful backhand drive.

See the strength of her arm, as firm and hairy as Hendren's;
   See the size of her thighs, the pout of her lips as, cross,
And full of a pent-up strength, she swipes at the rhododendron
      Lucky the rhododendrons,
      And flings her arrogant love-lock
   Back with a petulant toss.

Over the-redolent pinewoods, in at the bathroom casement,
   One fine Saturday, Windlesham bells shall call:
Up the Butterfield aisle rich with Gothic enlacement,
      Licensed now for embracement,
      Pam and I, as the organ
   Thunders over you all.

ON SEEING AN OLD POET
IN THE CAFÉ ROYAL

I saw him in the Café Royal.
  Very old and very grand.
Modernistic shone the lamplight
  There in London's fairyland.
'Devilled chicken. Devilled whitebait.
  Devil if I understand.

Where is Oscar? Where is Bosie?
  Have I seen that man before?
And the old one in the corner,
  Is it really Wratislaw?'
Scent of Tutti-Frutti-Sen-Sen
  And cheroots upon the floor.

PARLIAMENT HILL FIELDS

Rumbling under blackened girders, Midland, bound for
                                    Cricklewood,
Puffed its sulphur to the sunset where that Land of Laundries
                                    stood.
Rumble under, thunder over, train and tram alternate go,
Shake the floor and smudge the ledger, Charrington, Sells,
                                    Dale and Co.,
Nuts and nuggets in the window, trucks along the lines below.

When the Bon Marché was shuttered, when the feet were hot
                                    and tired,
Outside Charrington's we waited, by the 'STOP HERE IF
                                    REQUIRED',
Launched aboard the shopping basket, sat precipitately down,
Rocked past Zwanziger the baker's, and the terrace blackish
                                    brown,
And the curious Anglo-Norman parish church of Kentish
                                    Town.

Till the tram went over thirty, sighting terminus again,
Past municipal lawn tennis and the bobble-hanging plane;
Soft the light suburban evening caught our ashlar-speckled
                                    spire,
Eighteen-sixty Early English, as the mighty elms retire
Either side of Brookfield Mansions flashing fine
                                    French-window fire.

Oh the after-tram-ride quiet, when we heard a mile beyond,
Silver music from the bandstand, barking dogs by Highgate
                                    Pond;
Up the hill where stucco houses in Virginia creeper drown –
And my childish wave of pity, seeing children carrying down
Sheaves of drooping dandelions to the courts of Kentish Town.

SENEX

Oh would I could subdue the flesh
   Which sadly troubles me!
And then perhaps could view the flesh
As though I never knew the flesh
   And merry misery.

To see the golden hiking girl
   With wind about her hair,
The tennis-playing, biking girl,
The wholly-to-my-liking girl,
   To see and not to care.

At sundown on my tricycle
   I tour the Borough's edge,
And icy as an icicle
See bicycle by bicycle
   Stacked waiting in the hedge.

Get clown from me! I thunder there,
   You spaniels! Shut your jaws!
Your teeth are stuffed with underwear,
Suspenders torn asunder there
   And buttocks in your paws!

Oh whip the dogs away my Lord,
   They make me ill with lust.
Bend bare knees down to pray, my Lord,
Teach sulky lips to say, my Lord,
   That flaxen hair is dust.

THE PLANSTER'S VISION

Cut down that timber! Bells, too many and strong,
  Pouring their music through the branches bare,
  From moon-white church-towers down the windy air
Have pealed the centuries out with Evensong.
Remove those cottages, a huddled throng!
  Too many babies have been born in there,
  Too many coffins, bumping down the stair,
Carried the old their garden paths along.

I have a Vision of The Future, chum,
  The workers' flats in fields of soya beans
    Tower up like silver pencils, score on score:
And Surging Millions hear the Challenge come
  From microphones in communal canteens
    'No Right! No Wrong! All's perfect, evermore.'

IN A BATH TEASHOP

'Let us not speak, for the love we bear one another –
　　Let us hold hands and look.'
She, such a very ordinary little woman;
　　He, such a thumping crook;
But both, for a moment, little lower than the angels
　　In the teashop's ingle-nook.

HYMN

The Church's Restoration
  In eighteen-eighty-three
Has left for contemplation
  Not what there used to be.
How well the ancient woodwork
  Looks round the Rect'ry hall,
Memorial of the good work
  Of him who plann'd it all.

He who took down the pew-ends
  And sold them anywhere
But kindly spared a few ends
  Work'd up into a chair.
O worthy persecution
  Of dust! O hue divine!
O cheerful substitution,
  Thou varnishéd pitch-pine!

Church furnishing! Church furnishing!
  Sing art and crafty praise!
He gave the brass for burnishing
  He gave the thick red baize,
He gave the new addition,
  Pull'd down the dull old aisle,
– To pave the sweet transition
  He gave th' encaustic tile.

Of marble brown and veinéd
  He did the pulpit make;
He order'd windows stainéd
  Light red and crimson lake.
Sing on, with hymns uproarious,
  Ye humble and aloof,
Look up! and oh how glorious
  He has restored the roof!

HUNTER TRIALS

It's awf'lly bad luck on Diana,
    Her ponies have swallowed their bits;
She fished down their throats with a spanner
    And frightened them all into fits.

So now she's attempting to borrow.
    Do lend her some bits, Mummy, *do*;
I'll lend her my own for to-morrow,
    But to-day *I*'ll be wanting them too.

Just look at Prunella on Guzzle,
    The wizardest pony on earth;
Why doesn't she slacken his muzzle
    And tighten the breech in his girth?

I say, Mummy, there's Mrs. Geyser
    And doesn't she look pretty sick?
I bet it's because Mona Lisa
    Was hit on the hock with a brick.

Miss Blewitt says Monica threw it,
    But Monica says it was Joan,
And Joan's very thick with Miss Blewitt,
    So Monica's sulking alone.

And Margaret failed in her paces,
    Her withers got tied in a noose,
So her coronets caught in the traces
    And now all her fetlocks are loose.

Oh, it's me now. I'm terribly nervous.
   I wonder if Smudges will shy.
She's practically certain to swerve as
   Her Pelham is over one eye.

*   *   *   *   *

Oh wasn't it naughty of Smudges?
   Oh, Mummy, I'm sick with disgust.
She threw me in front of the Judges,
   And my silly old collarbone's bust.

INVASION EXERCISE ON
THE POULTRY FARM

Softly croons the radiogram, loudly hoot the owls,
Judy gives the door a slam and goes to feed the fowls.
Marty rolls a Craven A around her ruby lips
And runs her yellow fingers down her corduroyed hips,
Shuts her mouth and screws her eyes and puffs her fag alight
And hears some most peculiar cries that echo through the night.
Ting-a-ling the telephone, to-whit to-whoo the owls,
Judy, Judy, Judy girl, and have you fed the fowls?
No answer as the poultry gate is swinging there ajar.
Boom the bombers overhead, between the clouds a star,
And just outside, among the arks, in a shadowy sheltered place
Lie Judy and a paratroop in horrible embrace.
Ting-a-ling the telephone. 'Yes, this is Marty Hayne.'
'Have you seen a paratroop come walking down your lane?
He may be on your premises, he may be somewhere near,
And if he is report the fact to Major Maxton-Weir.'
Marty moves in dread towards the window – standing there
Draws the curtain – sees the guilty movement of the pair.[1]
White with rage and lined with age but strong and sturdy still
Marty now co-ordinates her passions and her will,
She will teach that Judy girl to trifle with the heart
And go and kiss a paratroop like any common tart.
She switches up the radiogram and covered by the blare
She goes and gets a riding whip and whirls it in the air,
She fetches down a length of rope and rushes, breathing hard
To let the couple have it for embracing in the yard.
Crack! the pair are paralysed. Click! they cannot stir.
Zip! she's trussed the paratroop. There's no embracing *her*.
'Hullo, hullo, hullo, hullo . . . Major Maxton-Weir?
I've trussed your missing paratroop. He's waiting for you here.'

[1] These lines in italic are by Henry Oscar.

ON A PORTRAIT OF A DEAF MAN

The kind old face, the egg-shaped head,
  The tie, discreetly loud,
The loosely fitting shooting clothes,
  A closely fitting shroud.

He liked old City dining-rooms,
  Potatoes in their skin,
But now his mouth is wide to let
  The London clay come in.

He took me on long silent walks
  In country lanes when young,
He knew the name of ev'ry bird
  But not the song it sung.

And when he could not hear me speak
  He smiled and looked so wise
That now I do not like to think
  Of maggots in his eyes.

He liked the rain-washed Cornish air
  And smell of ploughed-up soil,
He liked a landscape big and bare
  And painted it in oil.

But least of all he liked that place
  Which hangs on Highgate Hill
Of soaked Carrara-covered earth
  For Londoners to fill.

He would have liked to say good-bye,
  Shake hands with many friends,
In Highgate now his finger-bones
  Stick through his finger-ends.

You, God, who treat him thus and thus,
  Say 'Save his soul and pray.'
You ask me to believe You and
  I only see decay.

INDOOR GAMES NEAR NEWBURY

In among the silver birches winding ways of tarmac wander
  And the signs to Bussock Bottom, Tussock Wood and.
                                      Windy Brake,
Gabled lodges, tile-hung churches, catch the lights of our
                                      Lagonda
  As we drive to Wendy's party, lemon curd and Christmas
                                      cake.

        Rich the makes of motor whirring,
        Past the pine-plantation purring
            Come up, Hupmobile, Delage!
        Short the way your chauffeurs travel,
        Crunching over private gravel
          Each from out his warm garáge.

Oh but Wendy, when the carpet yielded to my indoor pumps
        There you stood, your gold hair streaming,
        Handsome in the hall-light gleaming
There you looked and there you led me off into the game of
                                    clumps
        Then the new Victrola playing
        And your funny uncle saying
'Choose your partners for a fox-trot! Dance until its *tea*
                                  o'clock!
        'Come on, young 'uns, foot it featly!'
        Was it chance that paired us neatly,
        I, who loved you so completely,
You, who pressed me closely to you, hard against your party
                                  frock?'

'Meet me when you've finished eating!' So we met and no one
                                                        found us.
    Oh that dark and furry cupboard while the rest played hide
                                                        and seek!
Holding hands our two hearts beating in the bedroom silence
                                                        round us,
Holding hands and hardly hearing sudden footstep, thud and
                                                        shriek.

            Love that lay too deep for kissing –
            'Where *is* Wendy? Wendy's missing!'
                Love so pure *it had* to end,
            Love so strong that I was frighten'd
            When you gripped my fingers tight and
Hugging, whispered 'I'm your friend.'

Goodbye Wendy! Send the fairies, pinewood elf and larch tree
                                                        gnome,
            Spingle-spangled stars are peeping
            At the lush Lagonda creeping
Down the winding ways of tarmac to the leaded lights of
                                                        home.
            There, among the silver birches,
            All the bells of all the churches
Sounded in the bath-waste running out into the frosty air.
            Wendy speeded my undressing,
            Wendy is the sheet's caressing
            Wendy bending gives a blessing,
Holds me as I drift to dreamland, safe inside my slumber-wear.

YOUTH AND AGE ON
BEAULIEU RIVER, HANTS

Early sun on Beaulieu water
    Lights the undersides of oaks,
Clumps of leaves it floods and blanches,
All transparent glow the branches
    Which the double sunlight soaks;
To her craft on Beaulieu water
Clemency the General's daughter
    Pulls across with even strokes.

Schoolboy-sure she is this morning;
    Soon her sharpie's rigg'd and free.
Cool beneath a garden awning
    Mrs. Fairclough, sipping tea
And raising large long-distance glasses
As the little sharpie passes,
    Sighs our sailor girl to see:

Tulip figure, so appealing,
    Oval face, so serious-eyed,
Tree-roots pass'd and muddy beaches.
On to huge and lake-like reaches,
    Soft and sun-warm, see her glide –
Slacks the slim young limbs revealing,
Sun-brown arm the tiller feeling –
    With the wind and with the tide.

Evening light will bring the water,
    Day-long sun will burst the bud,
Clemency, the General's daughter,
    Will return upon the flood.
But the older woman only
Knows the ebb-tide leaves her lonely
    With the shining fields of mud.

ST. SAVIOUR'S, ABERDEEN PARK,
HIGHBURY, LONDON, N.

With oh such peculiar branching and over-reaching of wire
    Trolley-bus standards pick their threads from the London sky
Diminishing up the perspective, Highbury-bound retire
    Threads and buses and standards with plane trees volleying by
And, more peculiar still, that ever-increasing spire
    Bulges over the housetops, polychromatic and high.

Stop the trolley-bus, stop! And here, where the roads unite
    Of weariest worn-out London – no cigarettes, no beer,
No repairs undertaken, nothing in stock – alight;
    For over the waste of willow-herb, look at her, sailing clear,
A great Victorian church, tall, unbroken and bright
    In a sun that's setting in Willesden and saturating us here.

These were the streets my parents knew when they loved and
                                 won –
    The brougham that crunched the gravel, the laurel-girt paths
                              that wind,
Geranium-beds for the lawn, Venetian blinds for the sun,
    A separate tradesman's entrance, straw in the mews behind,
Just in the four-mile radius where hackney carriages run,
    Solid Italianate houses for the solid commercial mind.

These were the streets they knew; and I, by descent, belong
    To these tall neglected houses divided into flats.
Only the church remains, where carriages used to throng
    And my mother stepped out in flounces and my father
                            stepped out in spats
To shadowy stained-glass matins or gas-lit evensong
    And back in a country quiet with doffing of chimney hats.

Great red church of my parents, cruciform crossing they
                                                    knew –
   Over these same encaustics they and their parents trod
Bound through a red-brick transept for a once familiar pew
   Where the organ set them singing and the sermon let them
                                                    nod
And up this coloured brickwork the same long shadows grew
   As these in the stencilled chancel where I kneel in the
                                                    presence of God.

Wonder beyond Time's wonders, that Bread so white and
                                                    small
   Veiled in golden curtains, too mighty for men to see,
Is the Power which sends the shadows up this polychrome
                                                    wall,
   Is God who created the present, the chain-smoking millions
                                                    and me;
Beyond the throb of the engines is the throbbing heart of all –
   Christ, at this Highbury altar, I offer myself To Thee.

NORTH COAST RECOLLECTIONS

No people on the golf-links, not a crack
Of well-swung driver from the fourteenth tee,
No sailing bounding ball across the turf
And lady's slipper of the fairway. Black
Rises Bray Hill and, Stepper-wards, the sun
Sends Bray Hill's phantom stretching to the church.
The lane, the links, the beach, the cliffs are bare
The neighbourhood is dressing for a dance
And lamps are being lit in bungalows.
   O! thymy time of evening: clover scent
And feathery tamarisk round the churchyard wall
And shrivelled sea-pinks and this foreshore pale
With silver sand and sharpened quartz and slate
And brittle twigs, bleached, salted and prepared
For kindling blue-flamed fires on winter nights.
   Here Petroc landed, here I stand to-day;
The same Atlantic surges roll for me
As rolled for Parson Hawker and for him,
And spent their gathering thunder on the rocks
Crashing with pebbly backwash, burst again
And strewed the nibbled fields along the cliffs.

   When low tides drain the estuary gold
Small intersecting breakers far away
Ripple about a bar of shifting sand
Where centuries ago were waving woods
Where centuries hence, there will be woods again.

   Within the bungalow of Mrs. Hanks
Her daughter Phoebe now French-chalks the floor.
Norman and Gordon in their dancing pumps
Slide up and down, but can't make concrete smooth.
'My Sweet Hortense . . .'

Sings louder down the garden than the sea.
'A practice record, Phoebe. Mummykins,
Gordon and I will do the washing-up.'
'We picnic here; we scrounge and help ourselves,'
Says Mrs. Hanks, and visitors will smile
To see them all turn to it. Boys and girls
Weed in the sterile garden, mostly sand
And dead tomato-plants and chicken-runs.
To-day they cleaned the dulled Benares ware
(Dulled by the sea-mist), early made the beds,
And Phoebe twirled the icing round the cake
And Gordon tinkered with the gramophone
While into an immense enamel jug
Norman poured 'Eiffel Tower' for lemonade.

O! healthy bodies, bursting into 'teens
And bursting out of last year's summer clothes,
Fluff barking and French windows banging to
Till the asbestos walling of the place
Shakes with the life it shelters, and with all
The preparations for this evening's dance.

★   ★   ★

Four macrocarpa hide the tennis club.
Two children of a chartered actuary
(Beaworthy, Trouncer, Heppelwhite and Co.),
Harold and Bonzo Trouncer are engaged
In semi-finals for the tournament.
'Love thirty!' Pang! across the evening air
Twangs Harold's racquet. Plung! the ball returns.
Experience at Budleigh Salterton
Keeps Bonzo steady at the net. 'Well done!'
'Love forty!' Captain Mycroft, midst applause,
Pronounces for the Trouncers, to be sure
He can't be certain Bonzo didn't reach
A shade across the net, but Demon Sex,

That tulip figure in white cotton dress,
Bare legs, wide eyes and so tip-tilted nose
Quite overset him. Harold serves again
And Mrs. Pardon says it's getting cold,
Miss Myatt shivers, Lady Lambourn thinks
These English evenings are a little damp
And dreams herself again in fair Shanghai.
'Game . . . AND! and thank you!'; so the pair from Rock
(A neighbouring and less exclusive place)
Defeated, climb into their Morris Ten.
'The final is to-morrow! Well, good night!'
He lay in wait, he lay in wait, he did,
John Lambourn, curly-headed; dewy grass
Dampened his flannels, but he still remained.

The sunset drained the colours black and gold,
From his all-glorious First Eleven scarf.
But still he waited by the twilit hedge.
Only his eyes blazed blue with early love,
Blue blazing in the darkness of the lane,
Blue blazer, less incalculably blue,
Dark scarf, white flannels, supple body still,
First love, first light, first life. A heartbeat noise!
His heart or little feet? A snap of twigs
Dry, dead and brown the under branches part
And Bonzo scrambles by their secret way.
First love so deep, John Lambourn cannot speak,
So deep, he feels a tightening in his throat,
So tender, he could brush away the sand
Dried up in patches on her freckled legs,
Could hold her gently till the stars went down,
And if she cut herself would staunch the wound,
Yes, even with this First Eleven scarf,
And hold it there for hours.
So happy, and so deep he loves the world,
Could worship God and rocks and stones and trees,

Be nicer to his mother, kill himself
If that would make him pure enough for her.
And so at last he manages to say
'You going to the Hanks's hop to-night?'
'Well, I'm not sure. Are you?' 'I think I may –
'It's pretty dud though, – only lemonade.'

Sir Gawaint was a right and goodly knight
Nor ever wist he to uncurtis be.
So old, so lovely, and so very true!
Then Mrs. Wilder shut the Walter Crane
And tied the tapes and tucked her youngest in
What time without amidst the lavender
At late last 'He' played Primula and Prue
With new-found liveliness, for bed was soon.
And in the garage, serious seventeen
Harvey, the eldest, hammered on, content,
Fixing a mizzen to his model boat.
'Coo-ee! Coo-ee!' across the lavender,
Across the mist of pale gypsophila
And lolling purple poppies, Mumsie called,
A splendid sunset lit the rocking-horse
And Morris pattern of the nursery walls.
'Coo-ee!' the slate-hung, goodly-builded house
And sunset-sodden garden fell to quiet.
'Prue! Primsie! Mumsie wants you. Sleepi-byes!'
Prue jumped the marigolds and hid herself,
Her sister scampered to the Wendy Hut
And Harvey, glancing at his Ingersoll,
Thought 'Damn! I must get ready for the dance.'

So on this after-storm-lit evening
To Jim the raindrops in the tamarisk,
The fuchsia bells, the sodden matchbox lid
That checked a tiny torrent in the lane
Were magnified and shining clear with life.
Then pealing out across the estuary

The Padstow bells rang up for practice-night
An undersong to birds and dripping shrubs.
The full Atlantic at September spring
Flooded a final tide-mark up the sand,
And ocean sank to silence under bells,
And the next breaker was a lesser one
Then lesser still. Atlantic, bells and birds
Were layer on interchanging layers of sound.

THE OLYMPIC GIRL

The sort of girl I like to see
Smiles down from her great height at me.
She stands in strong, athletic pose
And wrinkles her *retroussé* nose.
Is it distaste that makes her frown,
So furious and freckled, down
On an unhealthy worm like me?
Or am I what she likes to see?
I do not know, though much I care.
εἴθε γενῃίοην . . . would I were
(Forgive me, shade of Rupert Brooke)
An object fit to claim her look.
Oh! would I were her racket press'd
With hard excitement to her breast.
And swished into the sunlit air
Arm-high above her tousled hair,
And banged against the bounding ball
'Oh! Plung!' my tauten'd strings would call,
'Oh! Plung! my darling, break my strings
For you I will do brilliant things.'
And when the match is over, I
Would flop beside you, hear you sigh;
And then, with what supreme caress,
You'ld tuck me up into my press.
Fair tigress of the tennis courts,
So short in sleeve and strong in shorts,
Little, alas, to you I mean,
For I am bald and old and green.

A LINCOLNSHIRE CHURCH

Greyly tremendous the thunder
Hung over the width of the wold
But here the green marsh was alight
In a huge cloud cavern of gold,
And there, on a gentle eminence,
Topping some ash trees, a tower
Silver and brown in the sunlight,
Worn by sea-wind and shower,
Lincolnshire Middle Pointed.
And around it, turning their backs,
The usual sprinkle of villas
The usual woman in slacks,
Cigarette in her mouth,
Regretting Americans, stands
As a wireless croons in the kitchen
Manicuring her hands.
Dear old, bloody old England
Of telegraph poles and tin,
Seemingly so indifferent
And with so little soul to win.
What sort of church, I wonder?
The path is a grassy mat,
And grass is drowning the headstones
Sloping this way and that.
'Cathedral Glass' in the windows,
A roof of unsuitable slate –
Restored with a vengeance, for certain,
About eighteen-eighty-eight.
The door swung easily open
(Unlocked, for these parts, is odd)
And there on the South aisle altar
Is the tabernacle of God.
There where the white light flickers

By the white and silver veil,
A wafer dipped in a wine-drop
Is the Presence the angels hail,
Is God who created the Heavens
And the wide green marsh as well
Who sings in the sky with the skylark
Who calls in the evening bell,
Is God who prepared His coming
With fruit of the earth for his food
With stone for building His churches
And trees for making His rood.
There where the white light flickers,
Our Creator is with us yet,
To be worshipped by you and the woman
Of the slacks and the cigarette.

       *   *   *   *   *

The great door shuts, and lessens
That roar of churchyard trees
And the Presence of God Incarnate
Has brought me to my knees.
'I acknowledge my transgressions'
The well-known phrases rolled
With thunder sailing over
From the heavily clouded wold.
'And my sin is ever before me.'
There in the lighted East
He stood in that lowering sunlight,
An Indian Christian priest.
And why he was here in Lincolnshire
I neither asked nor knew,
Nor whether his flock was many
Nor whether his flock was few
I thought of the heaving waters
That bore him from sun glare harsh

Of some Indian Anglican Mission
To this green enormous marsh.
There where the white light flickers,
Here, as the rains descend,
The same mysterious Godhead
Is welcoming His friend.

SUNDAY MORNING,
KING'S CAMBRIDGE

File into yellow candle light, fair choristers of King's
   Lost in the shadowy silence of canopied Renaissance stalls
In blazing glass above the dark glow skies and thrones and
                                                   wings
   Blue, ruby, gold and green between the whiteness of the
                                                   walls
And with what rich precision the stonework soars and springs
   To fountain out a spreading vault – a shower that never falls.

The white of windy Cambridge courts, the cobbles brown and
                                                 dry,
   The gold of plaster Gothic with ivy overgrown,
The apple-red, the silver fronts, the wide green flats and high.
   The yellowing elm-trees circled out on islands of their own –
Oh, here behold all colours change that catch the flying sky,
   To waves of pearly light that heave along the shafted stone.

In far East Anglian churches, the clasped hands lying long
   Recumbent on sepulchral slabs or effigied in brass
Buttress with prayer this vaulted roof so white and light and
                                               strong
   And countless congregations as the generations pass
Join choir and great crowned organ case, in centuries of song
   To praise Eternity contained in Time and coloured glass.

THE EMPTY PEW

Written on Penelope Betjeman's admission to the
Roman Catholic Church, 1948

In the perspective of Eternity
   The pain is nothing, now you go away
   Above the steaming thatch how silver-grey
Our chiming church tower, calling 'Come to me

My Sunday-sleeping villagers!' And she,
   Still half my life, kneels now with those who say
   'Take courage, daughter. Never cease to pray
God's grace will break him of his heresy.'

I, present with our Church of England few
   At the dear words of Consecration see
   The chalice lifted, hear the sanctus chime
And glance across to that deserted pew.
   In the Perspective of Eternity
   The pain is nothing – but, ah God, in Time.

LONGFELLOW'S VISIT TO VENICE
(To be read in a quiet New England accent)

Near the celebrated Lido where the breeze is fresh and free
Stands the ancient port of Venice called the City of the Sea.

All its streets are made of water, all its homes are brick and stone,
Yet it has a picturesqueness which is justly all its own.

Here for centuries have artists come to see the vistas quaint,
Here Bellini set his easel, here he taught his School to paint.

Here the youthful Giorgione gazed upon the domes and towers,
And interpreted his era in a way which pleases ours.

A later artist, Tintoretto, also did his paintings here,
Massive works which generations have continued to revere.

Still to-day come modern artists to portray the buildings fair
And their pictures may be purchased on San Marco's famous
                                                    Square.

When the bell notes from the belfries and the campaniles chime
Still to-day we find Venetians elegantly killing time

In their gilded old palazzos, while the music in our ears
Is the distant band at Florians mixed with songs of gondoliers.

Thus the New World meets the Old World and the sentiments
                                                    expressed
Are melodiously mingled in my warm New England breast.

THE LICORICE FIELDS
AT PONTEFRACT

In the licorice fields at Pontefract
    My love and I did meet
And many a burdened licorice bush
    Was blooming round our feet;
Red hair she had and golden skin,
Her sulky lips were shaped for sin,
Her sturdy legs were flannel-slack'd,
The strongest legs in Pontefract.

The light and dangling licorice flowers
    Gave off the sweetest smells;
From various black Victorian towers
    The Sunday evening bells
Came pealing over dales and hills
And tanneries and silent mills
And lowly streets where country stops
And little shuttered corner shops.

She cast her blazing eyes on me
    And plucked a licorice leaf;
I was her captive slave and she
    My red-haired robber chief.
Oh love! for love I could not speak,
It left me winded, wilting, weak
And held in brown arms strong and bare
And wound with flaming ropes of hair.

N.W.5 & N.6

Red cliffs arise. And up them service lifts
Soar with the groceries to silver heights.
Lissenden Mansions. And my memory sifts
Lilies from lily-like electric lights
And Irish stew smells from the smell of prams
And roar of seas from roar of London trams.

Out of it all my memory carves the quiet
Of that dark privet hedge where pleasures breed,
There first, intent upon its leafy diet,
I watched the looping caterpillar feed
And saw it hanging in a gummy froth
Till, weeks on, from the chrysalis burst the moth.

I see black oak twigs outlined on the sky,
Red squirrels on the Burdett-Coutts estate.
I ask my nurse the question 'Will I die?'
As bells from sad St. Anne's ring out so late,
'And if I do die, will I go to Heaven?'
Highgate at eventide. Nineteen-eleven.

'You will. I won't.' From that cheap nursery-maid,
Sadist and puritan as now I see,
I first learned what it was to be afraid,
Forcibly fed when sprawled across her knee
Lock'd into cupboards, left alone all day,
'World without end.' What fearsome words to pray.

'World without end.' It was not what she'ld do
That frightened me so much as did her fear
And guilt at endlessness. I caught them too,
Hating to think of sphere succeeding sphere
Into eternity and God's dread will.
I caught her terror then. I have it still.

HUXLEY HALL

In the Garden City Café with its murals on the wall
Before a talk on 'Sex and Civics' I meditated on the Fall.

Deep depression settled on me under that electric glare
While outside the lightsome poplars flanked the rose-beds in
the square.

While outside the carefree children sported in the summer haze
And released their inhibitions in a hundred different ways.

She who eats her greasy crumpets snugly in the inglenook
Of some birch-enshrouded homestead, dropping butter on her
book

Can she know the deep depression of this bright, hygienic hell?
And her husband, stout free-thinker, can he share in it as well?

Not the folk-museum's charting of man's Progress out of slime
Can release me from the painful seeming accident of Time.

Barry smashes Shirley's dolly, Shirley's eyes are crossed with hate,
Comrades plot a Comrade's downfall 'in the interests of the State'.

Not my vegetarian dinner, not my lime-juice minus gin,
Quite can drown a faint conviction that we may be born in Sin.

CHRISTMAS

The bells of waiting Advent ring,
    The Tortoise stove is lit again
And lamp-oil light across the night
    Has caught the streaks of winter rain
In many a stained-glass window sheen
From Crimson Lake to Hooker's Green.

The holly in the windy hedge
    And round the Manor House the yew,
Will soon be stripped to deck the ledge,
    The altar, font and arch and pew,
So that the villagers can say
'The church looks nice' on Christmas Day.

Provincial public houses blaze
    And Corporation tramcars clang,
On lighted tenements I gaze
    Where paper decorations hang,
And bunting in the red Town Hall
Says 'Merry Christmas to you all.'

And London shops on Christmas Eve
    Are strung with silver bells and flowers
As hurrying clerks the City leave
    To pigeon-haunted classic towers,
And marbled clouds go scudding by
The many-steepled London sky.

And girls in slacks remember Dad,
     And oafish louts remember Mum,
And sleepless children's hearts are glad,
     And Christmas-morning bells say 'Come!'
Even to shining ones who dwell
Safe in the Dorchester Hotel.

And is it true? And is it true,
     This most tremendous tale of all,
Seen in a stained-glass window's hue,
     A Baby in an ox's stall?
The Maker of the stars and sea
Become a Child on earth for me?

And is it true? For if it is,
     No loving fingers tying strings
Around those tissued fripperies,
     The sweet and silly Christmas things,
Bath salts and inexpensive scent
And hideous tie so kindly meant,

No love that in a family dwells,
     No carolling in frosty air,
Nor all the steeple-shaking bells
     Can with this single Truth compare –
That God was Man in Palestine
And lives to-day in Bread and Wine.

SEASIDE GOLF

How straight it flew, how long it flew,
  It clear'd the rutty track
And soaring, disappeared from view
  Beyond the bunker's back –
A glorious, sailing, bounding drive
That made me glad I was alive.

And down the fairway, far along
  It glowed a lonely white;
I played an iron sure and strong
  And clipp'd it out of sight,
And spite of grassy banks between
I knew I'd find it on the green.

And so I did. It lay content
  Two paces from the pin;
A steady putt and then it went
  Oh, most securely in.
The very turf rejoiced to see
That quite unprecedented three.

Ah! seaweed smells from sandy caves
  And thyme and mist in whiffs,
In-coming tide, Atlantic waves
  Slapping the sunny cliffs,
Lark song and sea sounds in the air
And splendour, splendour everywhere.

MIDDLESEX

Gaily into Ruislip Gardens
    Runs the red electric train,
With a thousand Ta's and Pardon's
    Daintily alights Elaine;
Hurries down the concrete station
With a frown of concentration,
Out into the outskirt's edges
Where a few surviving hedges
Keep alive our lost Elysium – rural Middlesex again.

Well cut Windsmoor flapping lightly,
    Jacqmar scarf of mauve and green
Hiding hair which, Friday nightly,
    Delicately drowns in Drene;
Fair Elaine the bobby-soxer,
Fresh-complexioned with Innoxa,
Gains the garden – father's hobby –
Hangs her Windsmoor in the lobby,
Settles down to sandwich supper and the television screen.

Gentle Brent, I used to know you
    Wandering Wembley-wards at will,
Now what change your waters show you
    In the meadowlands you fill!
Recollect the elm-trees misty
And the footpaths climbing twisty
Under cedar-shaded palings,
Low laburnum-leaned-on railings,
Out of Northolt on and upward to the heights of Harrow hill.

Parish of enormous hayfields
   Perivale stood all alone,
And from Greenford scent of mayfields
   Most enticingly was blown
Over market gardens tidy,
Taverns for the *bona fide,*
Cockney anglers, cockney shooters,
Murray Poshes, Lupin Pooters
Long in Kensal Green and Highgate silent under soot and stone.

I. M.
WALTER RAMSDEN
OB. MARCH 26, 1947
PEMBROKE COLLEGE, OXFORD

Dr. Ramsden cannot read *The Times* obituary to-day
  He's dead.
Let monographs on silk worms by other people be
  Thrown away
  Unread
For he who best could understand and criticize them, he
  Lies clay
  In bed.

The body waits in Pembroke College where the ivy taps the
                       panes
  All night;
That old head so full of knowledge, that good heart that kept
                  the brains
  All right,
Those old cheeks that faintly flushed as the port suffused the
                      veins,
  Drain'd white.

Crocus in the Fellows' Garden, winter jasmine up the wall
  Gleam gold.
Shadows of Victorian chimneys on the sunny grassplot fall
  Long, cold.
Master, Bursar, Senior Tutor, these, his three survivors, all
  Feel old.

They remember, as the coffin to its final obsequations
    Leaves the gates,
Buzz of bees in window boxes on their summer ministrations,
    Kitchen din,
    Cups and plates,
And the getting of bump suppers for the long-dead generations
    Coming in,
    From Eights.

NORFOLK

How did the Devil come? When first attack?
 These Norfolk lanes recall lost innocence,
The years fall off and find me walking back
 Dragging a stick along the wooden fence
Down this same path, where, forty years ago,
My father strolled behind me, calm and slow.

I used to fill my hand with sorrel seeds
 And shower him with them from the tops of stiles,
I used to butt my head into his tweeds
 To make him hurry down those languorous miles
Of ash and alder-shaded lanes, till here
Our moorings and the masthead would appear.

There after supper lit by lantern light
 Warm in the cabin I could lie secure
And hear against the polished sides at night
 The lap lap lapping of the weedy Bure,
A whispering and watery Norfolk sound
Telling of all the moonlit reeds around.

How did the Devil come? When first attack?
 The church is just the same, though now I know
Fowler of Louth restored it. Time, bring back
 The rapturous ignorance of long ago,
The peace, before the dreadful daylight starts,
Of unkept promises and broken hearts.

LATE-FLOWERING LUST

My head is bald, my breath is bad,
    Unshaven is my chin,
I have not now the joys I had
    When I was young in sin.

I run my fingers down your dress
    With brandy-certain aim
And you respond to my caress
    And maybe feel the same.

But I've a picture of my own
    On this reunion night,
Wherein two skeletons are shewn
    To hold each other tight;

Dark sockets look on emptiness
    Which once was loving-eyed,
The mouth that opens for a kiss
    Has got no tongue inside.

I cling to you inflamed with fear
    As now you cling to me,
I feel how frail you are my dear
    And wonder what will be –

A week? or twenty years remain?
    And then – what kind of death?
A losing fight with frightful pain
    Or a gasping fight for breath?

Too long we let our bodies cling,
    We cannot hide disgust
At all the thoughts that in us spring
    From this late-flowering lust.

STATION SYREN

She sat with a Warwick Deeping,
    Her legs curl'd round in a ring,
Like a beautiful panther sleeping,
    Yet always ready to spring.

Tweed on her well-knit torso,
    Silk on each big strong leg,
An officer's lady – and more so
    Than those who buy off the peg.

More cash than she knew of for spending
    As a Southgate girl at home,
For there's crooning and clinging unending
    For the queen of the girls at the 'drome.

Beautiful brown eyes burning
    Deep on the Deeping page,
Beautiful dark hair learning
    Coiffuring tricks of the age.

Negligent hand for holding
    A Flight-Lieutenant at bay,
Petulant lips for scolding
    And kissing the trouble away.

But she isn't exactly partial
    To any of that sort of thing,
So maybe the Air Vice-Marshal
    Will buy her a Bravington ring.

ORIGINAL SIN ON THE SUSSEX COAST

Now on this out of season afternoon
Day schools which cater for the sort of boy
Whose parents go by Pullman once a month
To do a show in town, pour out their young
Into the sharply red October light.
Here where The Drive and Buckhurst Road converge
I watch the rival gangs and am myself
A schoolboy once again in shivering shorts.
I see the dust of sherbet on the chin
Of Andrew Knox well-dress'd, well-born, well-fed,
Even at nine a perfect gentleman,
Willie Buchanan waiting at his side –
Another Scot, eruptions on his skin.
I hear Jack Drayton whistling from the fence
Which hides the copper domes of 'Cooch Behar'.
That was the signal. So there's no escape.
A race for Willow Way and jump the hedge
Behind the Granville Bowling Club? Too late.
They'll catch me coming out in Seapink Lane.
Across the Garden of Remembrance? No,
That would be blasphemy and bring bad luck.
Well then, I'm *for* it. Andrew's at me first,
He pinions me in that especial grip
His brother learned in Kobë from a Jap
(No chance for me against the Japanese).
Willie arrives and winds me with a punch
Plum in the tummy, grips the other arm.
'You're to be booted. Hold him steady, chaps!'
A wait for taking aim. Oh trees and sky!
Then crack against the column of my spine,
Blackness and breathlessness and sick with pain
I stumble on the asphalt. Off they go
Away, away, thank God, and out of sight

So that I lie quite still and climb to sense
Too out of breath and strength to make a sound.
   Now over Polegate vastly sets the sun;
Dark rise the Downs from darker looking elms,
And out of Southern railway trains to tea
Run happy boys down various Station Roads,
Satchels of homework jogging on their backs,
So trivial and so healthy in the shade
Of these enormous Downs. And when they're home,
When the Post-Toasties mixed with Golden Shred
Make for the kiddies such a scrumptious feast,
Does Mum, the Persil-user, still believe
That there's no Devil and that youth is bliss?
As certain as the sun behind the Downs
And quite as plain to see, the Devil walks.

SUN AND FUN
SONG OF A NIGHT-CLUB PROPRIETRESS

I walked into the night-club in the morning;
　　There was kummel on the handle of the door.
The ashtrays were unemptied,
The cleaning unattempted,
　　And a squashed tomato sandwich on the floor.

I pulled aside the thick magenta curtains
　　– So Regency, so Regency, my dear –
And a host of little spiders
Ran a race across the ciders
　　To a box of baby 'pollies by the beer.

Oh sun upon the summer-going by-pass
　　Where ev'rything is speeding to the sea,
And wonder beyond wonder
That here where lorries thunder
　　The sun should ever percolate to me.

When Boris used to call in his Sedanca,
　　When Teddy took me down to his estate
When my nose excited passion,
When my clothes were in the fashion,
　　When my beaux were never cross if I was late,

There was sun enough for lazing upon beaches,
　　There was fun enough for far into the night.
But I'm dying now and done for,
What on earth was all the fun for?
　　For I'm old and ill and terrified and tight.

IN THE PUBLIC GARDENS

In the Public Gardens,
    To the airs of Strauss,
Eingang we're in love again
    When *ausgang* we were *aus*.

The waltz was played, the songs were sung,
    The night resolved our fears;
From bunchy boughs the lime trees hung
    Their gold electroliers.

Among the loud Americans
    Zwei Engländer were we,
You so white and frail and pale
    And me so deeply me;

I bought for you a dark-red rose,
    I saw your grey-green eyes,
As high above the floodlights,
    The true moon sailed the skies.

In the Public Gardens,
    Ended things begin;
Ausgang we were out of love
    Und eingang we are in.

UFFINGTON

Tonight we feel the muffled peal
   Hang on the village like a pall;
It overwhelms the towering elms –
   That death-reminding dying fall;
The very sky no longer high
   Comes down within the reach of all.
Imprisoned in a cage of sound
Even the trivial seems profound.

DEVONSHIRE STREET W.1

The heavy mahogany door with its wrought-iron screen
  Shuts. And the sound is rich, sympathetic, discreet.
The sun still shines on this eighteenth-century scene
  With Edwardian faience adornments – Devonshire Street.

No hope. And the X-ray photographs under his arm
  Confirm the message. His wife stands timidly by.
The opposite brick-built house looks lofty and calm
  Its chimneys steady against a mackerel sky.

No hope. And the iron nob of this palisade
  So cold to the touch, is luckier now than he
'Oh merciless, hurrying Londoners! Why was I made
  For the long and the painful deathbed coming to me?'

She puts her fingers in his as, loving and silly,
  At long-past Kensington dances she used to do
'It's cheaper to take the tube to Piccadilly
  And then we can catch a nineteen or a twenty-two.'

A RUSSELL FLINT

I could not speak for amazement at your beauty
　　As you came, down the Garrick stair,
Grey-green eyes like the turbulent Atlantic
　　And floppy schoolgirl hair.

I could see you in a Sussex teashop,
　　Dressed in peasant weave and brogues,
Turning over, as firelight shone on brassware,
　　Last year's tea-stained *Vogues*.

I could see you as a large-eyed student,
　　Frowning as you tried to learn,
Or, head flung back, the confident girl prefect,
　　Thrillingly kind and stern.

I could not speak for amazement at your beauty;
　　Yet when you spoke to me,
You were calm and gentle as a rock pool
　　Waiting, warm, for the sea.

Wave on wave, I plunged in them to meet you –
　　In wave on wave I drown;
Calm rock pool, on the shore of my security
　　Hold me when the tide goes down.

AGRICULTURAL CARESS

Keep me from Thelma's sister Pearl!
She puts my senses in a whirl,
Weakens my knees and keeps me waiting
Until my heart stops palpitating.

The debs may turn disdainful backs
On Pearl's uncouth mechanic slacks,
And outraged see the fire that lies
And smoulders in her long-lashed eyes.

Have they such weather-freckled features,
The smooth sophisticated creatures?
Ah, not to them such limbs belong,
Such animal movements sure and strong,

Such arms to take a man and press
In agricultural caress
His head to hers, and hold him there
Deep buried in her chestnut hair.

God shrive me from this morning lust
For supple farm girls: if you must,
Send the cold daughter of an earl –
But spare me Thelma's sister Pearl!

REMORSE

The lungs draw in the air and rattle it out again;
    The eyes revolve in their sockets and upwards stare;
No more worry and waiting and troublesome doubt again –
    She whom I loved and left is no longer there.

The nurse puts down her knitting and walks across to her,
    With quick professional eye she surveys the dead.
Just one patient the less and little the loss to her,
    Distantly tender she settles the shrunken head.

Protestant claims and Catholic, the wrong and the right of
                                     them,
    Unimportant they seem in the face of death –
But my neglect and unkindness – to lose the sight of them
    I would listen even again to that labouring breath.

MONODY ON THE DEATH OF
ALDERSGATE STREET STATION

Snow falls in the buffet of Aldersgate station,
   Soot hangs in the tunnel in clouds of steam.
City of London! before the next desecration
   Let your steepled forest of churches be my theme.

Sunday Silence! with every street a dead street,
   Alley and courtyard empty and cobbled mews,
Till 'tingle tang' the bell of St. Mildred's Bread Street
   Summoned the sermon taster to high box pews,

And neighbouring towers and spirelets joined the ringing
   With answering echoes from heavy commercial walls
Till all were drowned as the sailing clouds went singing
   On the roaring flood of a twelve-voiced peal from Paul's.

Then would the years fall off and Thames run slowly;
   Out into marshy meadow-land flowed the Fleet:
And the walled-in City of London, smelly and holy,
   Had a tinkling mass house in every cavernous street.

The bells rang down and St. Michael Paternoster
   Would take me into its darkness from College Hill,
Or Christ Church Newgate Street (with St. Leonard Foster)
   Would be late for Mattins and ringing insistent still.

Last of the east wall sculpture, a cherub gazes
   On broken arches, rosebay, bracken and dock,
Where once I heard the roll of the Prayer Book phrases
   And the sumptuous tick of the old west gallery clock.

Snow falls in the buffet of Aldersgate station,
   Toiling and doomed from Moorgate Street puffs the train,
For us of the steam and the gas-light, the lost generation,
   The new white cliffs of the City are built in vain.

HARVEST HYMN

We spray the fields and scatter
    The poison on the ground
So that no wicked wild flowers
    Upon our farm be found.
We like whatever helps us
    To line our purse with pence;
The twenty-four-hour broiler-house
    And neat electric fence.

All concrete sheds around us
    And Jaguars in the yard,
The telly lounge and deep-freeze
    Are ours from working hard.

We fire the fields for harvest,
    The hedges swell the flame,
The oak trees and the cottages
    From which our fathers came.
We give no compensation,
    The earth is ours today,
And if we lose on arable,
    Then bungalows will pay.

All concrete sheds . . . etc.

MONODY ON THE DEATH OF A
PLATONIST BANK CLERK

This is the lamp where he first read Whitman
    Out of the library large and free.
Every quarter the bus to Kirkstall
    Stopped and waited, but on read he.

This was his room with books in plenty:
    Dusty, now I have raised the blind –
Fenimore Cooper, Ballantyne, Henty,
    Edward Carpenter wedged behind.

These are the walls adorned with portraits,
    Camera studies and Kodak snaps;
'Camp at Pevensey' – 'Scouts at Cleethorpes' –
    There he is with the lads and chaps.

This is the friend, the best and greatest,
    Pure in his surplice, smiling, true –
The enlarged Photomaton – that's the latest,
    Next to the coloured one 'August Blue'.

These are his pipes. Ah! how he loved them,
    Puffed and petted them, after walks,
After tea and a frowst with crumpets,
    Puffed the smoke into serious talks.

All the lot of them, how they came to him –
    Tea and chinwag – gay young lives!
Somehow they were never the same to him
    When they married and brought their wives.

CAPRICE

I sat only two tables off from the one I was sacked at,
        Just three years ago,
And here was another meringue like the one which I hacked at
        When pride was brought low
And the coffee arrived – the place which she had to use tact at
        For striking the blow.

'I'm making some changes next week in the organisation
        And though I admire
Your work for me, John, yet the need to increase circulation
        Means you must retire:
An outlook more global than yours is the qualification
        I really require.'

Oh sickness of sudden betrayal! Oh purblind Creator!
        Oh friendship denied!
I stood on the pavement and wondered which loss was the
                    greater –
        The cash or the pride.
Explanations to make to subordinates, bills to pay later
        Churned up my inside.

I fell on my feet. But what of those others, worse treated,
        Your memory's ghosts,
In gloomy bed-sitters in Fulham, ill-fed and unheated,
        Applying for posts?
Do they haunt their successors and you as you sit here
                    repleted
        With entrées and roasts?

HEARTS TOGETHER

How emerald the chalky depths
   Below the Dancing Ledge!
We pulled the jelly-fishes up
   And threw them in the hedge
That with its stones and sea-pink tufts
   Ran to the high cliff edge.

And lucky was the jelly-fish
   That melted in the sun
And poured its vitals on the turf
   In self-effacing fun,
Like us who in each other's arms
   Were seed and soul in one.

O rational the happy bathe
   An hour before our tea,
When you were swimming breast-stroke, all
   Along the rocking sea
And, in between the waves, explain'd
   The Universe to me.

The Dorset sun stream'd on our limbs
   And scorch'd our hinder parts:
We gazed into the pebble beach
   And so discussed the arts,
O logical and happy we
   Emancipated hearts.

AN EIGHTEENTH-CENTURY
CALVINISTIC HYMN

Thank God my Afflictions are such
    That I cannot lie down on my Bed,
And if I but take to my Couch
    I incessantly Vomit and Bleed.

I am not too sure of my Worth,
    Indeed it is tall as a Palm;
But what Fruits can it ever bring forth
    When Leprosy sits at the Helm?

Though Torment's the Soul's Goal's Rewards
    The contrary's Proof of my Guilt,
While Dancing, Backgammon and Cards,
    Are among the worst Symptoms I've felt.

Oh! I bless the good Lord for my Boils.
    For my mental and bodily pains,
For without them my Faith all congeals
    And I'm doomed to HELL'S NE'ER-ENDING FLAMES.

LENTEN THOUGHTS OF
A HIGH ANGLICAN

Isn't she lovely, 'the Mistress'?
    With her wide-apart grey-green eyes,
The droop of her lips and, when she smiles,
    Her glance of amused surprise?

How nonchalantly she wears her clothes,
    How expensive they, are as well!
And the sound of her voice is as soft and deep
    As the Christ Church tenor bell.

But why do I call her 'the Mistress'
    Who know not her way of life?
Because she has more of a cared-for air
    Than many a legal wife.

How elegantly she swings along
    In the vapoury incense veil;
The angel choir must pause in song
    When she kneels at the altar rail.

The parson said that we shouldn't stare
    Around when we come to church,
Or the Unknown God we are seeking
    May forever elude our search.

But I hope the preacher will not think
    It unorthodox and odd
If I add that I glimpse in 'the Mistress'
    A hint of the Unknown God.

[This is about a lady I see on Sunday mornings
in a London church.]

COUNTY

God save me from the Porkers,
   God save me from their sons,
Their noisy tweedy sisters
   Who follow with the guns,
The old and scheming mother,
   Their futures that she plann'd,
The ghastly younger brother
   Who married into land.

Their shots along the valley
   Draw blood out of the sky,
The wounded pheasants rally
   As hobnailed boots go by.
Where once the rabbit scampered
   The waiting copse is still
As Porker fat and pampered
   Comes puffing up the hill.

'A left and right! Well done, sir!
   They're falling in the road;
And here's your other gun, sir.'
   'Don't talk. You're here to load.'
He grabs his gun, not seeing
   A thing but birds in air,
And blows them out of being
   With self-indulgent stare.

Triumphant after shooting
   He still commands the scene,
His Land Rover comes hooting
   Beaters and dogs between.
Then dinner with a neighbour,
   It doesn't matter which,
Conservative or Labour,
   So long as he is rich.

A *faux bonhomme* and dull as well,
   All pedigree and purse,
We must admit that, though he's hell,
   His womenfolk are worse.
Bright in their county gin sets
   They tug their ropes of pearls
And smooth their tailored twin-sets
   And drop the names of earls.

Loud talk of meets and marriages
   And tax-evasion's heard
In many first-class carriages
   While servants travel third.
'My dear, I have to spoil them too –
   Or who would do the chores?
Well, here we are at Waterloo,
   I'll drop you at the Stores.'

God save me from the Porkers,
   The pathos of their lives,
The strange example that they set
   To new-rich farmers' wives
Glad to accept their bounty
   And worship from afar
And think of them as county –
   County is what they are.

THE LAST LAUGH

I made hay while the sun shone.
   My work sold.
Now, if the harvest is over
   And the world cold,
Give me the bonus of laughter
   As I lose hold.

INDEX OF FIRST LINES